THE LEGACY OF IGNORANTISM (IGNORANTISMO)

First published 1921
This edition published by Lector House in 2024

ISBN: 978-93-6138-474-5

Lector House LLP
Registered Office: H. No. 96, Block C, Tomar Colony,
Burari, Delhi – 110084, India
info@lectorhouse.com
www.lectorhouse.com

THE LEGACY OF IGNORANTISM (IGNORANTISMO)

TRINIDAD HERMENEGILDO PARDO DE TAVERA

2024

LECTOR HOUSE LLP

THE LEGACY OF IGNORANTISM (IGNORANTISMO)

An Address delivered before the Teachers Assembly, Baguio, April 23, 1920

BY

DR. T. H. PARDO DE TAVERA

Contents

Page

The Legacy of Ignorantism[1] *(Ignorantismo):*

An address[2] *delivered before the Teachers, Assembly, Baguio, April 23, 1920*

By Dr. T. H. Pardo de Tavera

> Woe unto you, lawyers! for ye have taken away the key of knowledge; ye entered not in yourselves, and them that were entering in ye hindered—Luke 11:52.

I have the honor to appear before you accepting with great pleasure an invitation which the Assistant Director, Mr. Osias, kindly extended to me. Having left the choice of the subject to my discretion, I deemed it worth while to speak on the Lay Education which has been in operation in our public schools since the implantation of the new régime which rules the destiny of the Filipino people. I am going to confine myself to facts, and shall speak as frankly and as faithfully as the case requires, altho in so doing I may hurt the feelings of some.

---

[1] *Ignorantism*, the spirit of those who extol the advantage of ignorance; obscurantism.

[2] Translated from Spanish.

Satisfying Movement

For some time in our society there has been a growing concern against immorality, against vice, against idleness; in short against those which can rightly be called social ills. Such a tendency is certainly good and satisfying; a sign of a notable social progress altho for the majority it is a cause of alarm and regret because of the seeming increase of such ills. Is there a positive increase of immorality? Is there real cause for alarm because of a moral retrogression of our society?

After having asked myself these questions and after having considered the bases for the public clamor and for the excited opinion before the sight of growing vice and immorality, I can say that this tendency of public opinion is satisfying—a sign of betterment, of progress of general morals. In other words, it is not immorality which is growing. Rather, it is the moral consciousness which is gaining ground in individual consciences, thus forming *a public opinion which formerly did not exist*, completely awake to existing social evils and which are combatted. Not that social morals has been decadent. On the contrary, a moral consciousness has been rapidly formed in our society, a consciousness which formerly was found only among an inconsiderable minority, and which resulted in the new movement against vice and immorality.

Public Opinion in Favor of Hygiene

To better understand this phenomenon and to explain it as it *really* is and not as it *apparently* exists, it is worth while to compare it with the appearance of a new sentiment which was formed since the implantation of the American régime: the *hygienic consciousness*. Formerly, hardly anybody spoke of the unsanitary conditions of Manila, and only a few in our society had a true idea of its deplorable state. Now that our individual education has enabled us to understand what hygiene is and its importance has been demonstrated, we have not only improved our sanitary condition but a collective sentiment equal to the sum total of the individual sentiments has been formed, and a public opinion in favor of hygiene has been established. Since this opinion grows more rapidly than sanitation itself in Manila, we see that every once in a while the Bureau of Health is censured to the point of attributing to its fault the increase of anti-hygienic conditions, when in reality what increases is the clamor for hygiene by virtue of the increase of the individuals who understand hygiene and demand strict application of its laws and principles.

Now public opinion denounces hygienic shortcomings which are incomparably less harmful than formerly, but which we view not in a *relative* but *absolute* manner. An unsanitary condition is denounced absolutely as an intolerable evil; relatively speaking our censure would be less severe if we bore in mind that a similar ill is not close at hand; we suffered in silence when we were ignorant not of its existence but of its effects upon health, so then for us it existed in a latent state and we did not see, feel, or notice it because of lack of preparation. It is identical to what happens when at the foot of a post charged with electric current is placed the sign: "Danger to life." Such a sign is practically useless and is no means of safety to the individual who does not know how to read. The one who can read knows the danger; he who does not read does not avail himself of the hygienic value of the danger signal.

Anti-Cockpit Campaign

Against the cockpit there is now a widespread campaign. This did not grow out of increased passion for the vice but out of the increased number of its enemies. None can say that cockfighting has increased; it is easy to prove that it has decreased; the number of days permitted by law is now insignificant compared with what it was a few years ago. Nevertheless, the campaign against cockfighting has increased precisely because the number of cockfighters has decreased. Exactly the same thing happened in card playing and horse-racing.

Nothing in particular would be said about this general movement in favor of social morality if the attitude of public opinion would not have that mistaken and dangerous bias which is given it by certain elements which at all times have been an obstacle to the instruction of the Filipino people. These elements, taking advantage of the preoccupation of public opinion to combat vice and purify public morals, instead of simply supporting this movement and strengthening it justifying its usefulness by the good itself which it seeks to accomplish, launches a political campaign which consists in alarming the people making them believe that immorality increases, that the social ills are growing, that national life itself is endangered thru the fault of the reformers as a result of the new régime in vogue in the Philippines since the loss of the past sovereignty. They take advantage of the current of public opinion in favor of public morals, to make it appear that the democratic form of the Government, the English language, the lay schools, coeducation, and Anglo-Saxon civilization are the causes of the supposed growth of immorality: Such is the program of certain people!

Our Enemies

Those who in a great measure are guilty to their nation for the misfortunes that befell the Filipino people that resorted to revolution and rebellion to free themselves from a régime opposed to their progress and happiness, forgetting their incapacity to fulfill the obligations which, in the name of their country, they assumed here and which were the causes of the political failure of the past colonization, they to-day wish to defend their interests in our country pursuing their policy which would only produce dissension among the Filipinos. Under the pretext of interesting themselves more than we do in our own welfare, considering us to be blind and incapable to know and distinguish the good from the bad, deeming us *eternal indios* of inferior mentality, they seek to take us whithersoever they will, where it suits them, thru the dark path where none see but they, they who guide or wish to guide the indio, the eternal child who ought to allow himself to be led!

In a foreign weekly published in Manila, we read the following: “Dedicated to the search of the enemies of the progress of the Filipinos, we find them in every bucket, in every cabaret; in the *peaceful invasion* of Japanese in the Philippines; in "panguingue," in billiard games, in the prevailing immorality in the theaters, in the novel, in the cinematograph and in the postal card; and above all and over all, in the *lay school*." He who thus expresses himself seeking to arouse Filipino hatred against the Japanese, to create suspicion first and trouble afterwards, is a stranger, and in the language in which he himself writes are written the theatrical works and the immoral novels that come to the Philippines.[3] In his language, too, were promulgated those laws and regulations in our country instituting cockfighting, lottery, billiard, created as sources of revenue for the State—things which we the Filipinos could not oppose in the old political régime without at the same time opposing the government itself which made vice a source of revenue and which, to increase its funds, had to encourage such vices, similar to opium in official smoking-rooms. Of the lay school we shall now speak presently.

The Work of Calumny and Hatred

Considering the nature of this campaign against our present day institutions, and painfully impressed by the great harm which this disastrous work of calumny, hatred, distrust and pessimism must have upon the progress and tranquillity of us, the Filipinos, I deem it my duty to speak when I am led to think that the limit has been reached by a document which came to my hands. It is no less than a circular which a high prelate directs to the curates of the parishes of his diocese, and which deals with public instruction.[4]

Hell Threat

The whole document is an attack against the Government schools, simply because in them the Catholic religion is not taught, threatening with

[3] Of the one hundred fifty-six books which the censorship of the Manila Customs refused entrance because they are obscene, five were printed in French and one hundred fifty-one in Spanish. In English, it is known, no obscene literature is found.

[4] From the Bishop of Cebu, dated November 19, 1919.

hell those parents who send their children to such schools. At the close it says as follows:

> As a first step, after you have let the parents see the social evils which result from a Godless school, such as crime against purity, murder, suicide, rapine and robbery, disobedience against civil and ecclesiastical authorities, in short, the corruption of customs, *all the seasoned fruit of those lay schools*, your reverences should influence them to declare, in writing or communications which they should address to us, to the government without euphemisms their irrevocable and decided will that Christian education be given them in the schools. We, for our part, will look after the sending of these petitions to the Legislature.

Machiavelic Accusation

"All the seasoned fruit of those lay schools" said the prelate referring to the crimes and the corruption of customs which he mentions! An accusation of such nature must be proven by him who accuses. The worst part of it is that such accusations are made and later with the recommendation that they be made to sink into heads of parents or heads of families. The faithful will consider as true the affirmations that come from the lips of their priests, so that such propaganda promotes in the worst manner a feeling against a government accused of fomenting criminality in its schools. The prelate does not enjoin violence; but at such times as these, violence naturally results from an adequate preparation of the popular conscience; and when a people believes that the Government, the educator no less, is the cause of the thieves, the murderers, the corruptors, a people is truly dead who does not seek to wipe out by any means such a government, especially if it is foreign, which corrupts its citizens.

Colossal Transformation

Fortunately, it can be said without fear of erring that such accusations are altogether false; and if there is anything in the Philippines which deserves the approval of all worthy conscience, something which merits not only the gratitude but the admiration of the Filipino people, it is the organization of public education implanted by the American people. There is not a single Filipino capable of reasoning who does not see and understand the colossal transformation which our entire people experienced by virtue of that lay education. Not only did the Government organize an efficient educational system, but it extended it throughout the Archipelago in such a general way that some European nations which continually cite the annals of history, would very much like it for themselves; not only do we the Filipinos find in our lay schools those elements necessary for our instruction and our education so that we can be useful individuals to ourselves, and coöperate in the administration of our public affairs, but the private schools of the old régime have changed, have improved, have been transformed, have been placed to the level where they should, *following the standard maintained by the Government*. To deny this is sheer blindness.

A Dominican School in Formosa

Only he who is blinded by passion is capable of making accusation against the lay school such as we have here reproduced, and against which the first to protest will likely be the Dominican friars in the Philippines whose mission in Formosa, has a girl's school for the Chinese and Japanese in the Capitol, Taihoku, which I visited on my trip to that island. Reverend Father Clemente Fernandez, a Dominican and the Apostolic Vicar of Formosa, did me the honor of accompanying me in visiting such a school, called *Beata Imelda*, situated in the barrio of Daitelei, in Taihoku. It is a beautiful school of which the Dominicans can justly be proud. But it was not the material or educational organization of the institution that impressed me so much as the absence of all religious images in the rooms, classes, halls, and other rooms used for and by the girls.

On my noticing the existence of so singular a case, Reverend Clemente Fernandez made it known to me that, among the conditions stipulated by the law of public instruction of Formosa, both for the government as well as the private schools, is the absolute prohibition of religious education and the presentation of images and objects of worship. This is therefore a lay school, a *godless school*, upon which should also fall the surprising accusation of a prelate who makes use of the liberty afforded him by our government to teach his religion in our schools, but abusing such right and attempting furthermore to impose his will upon the Government, accusing it of teaching homicide, theft, immorality, and corruption of customs in our schools.

Were We to Use the Same Procedure

There is no doubt that even under the Spanish régime we already knew of the existence in the Philippines of criminals condemned to death and imprisonment for murder, theft, rape, sacrilege, and all kinds of crimes, and that the corruption of customs was neither unknown nor rare. Since under the entire period of Spanish domination, instruction was under the exclusive care of the friars of the Roman Church, if we utilize the same procedure of the above-mentioned prelate, we could also accuse all the priests of having instructed the Filipinos, thru their education, in murder and in theft, and that the corruption of customs was "all the seasoned fruit of the Catholic schools." I do not propose such an accusation; I only content myself with presenting it as a logical consequence which could be deduced following the method used by the prelate in speaking to no less than his priests in a circular designed to orient the mentality of his clergy and of his parishioners. Pondering over the accusation of the Bishop, it occurred to me that it would be beneficial to recall the public instruction that was formerly given in the Philippines by the "godly schools" and consider the results obtained. Confident in the respectable character, and, to many, the sacred character of the priests, I must resort to their testimony to know what that education was and what results it gave to the Filipino people.

We should not conceal the truth when the truth portrays things that may not be pleasing to us. None like those who are dedicated to instruction have such an interest in knowing the mentality of the society in which they live and which it is their duty to educate. An exact knowledge of the moral, intellectual, and physical defects of a people is the most important factor to orient its education, and it would be absurd to close one's eyes to what is bad, because the principle of correcting a certain thing is to know if it is a mistake or not. One cannot correct an evil of which he is ignorant.

The Education of the Filipino People under Religious Direction

Before attacking or defending the lay education of the public schools it would seem useful to know what the education of the Filipino people was under religious direction, and then know what results were obtained; that is to say, how a man subjected to such a system was transformed after more than three centuries of such a practice.

I must secure the data which I here present from ecclesiastical sources because, altho they contain a certain exaggeration, in speaking of its own work which, as it is natural, they defend, magnify, and praise, they are after all the most useful in knowing the defects themselves which, under the circumstances, constitute real confessions.

Father Santiago Paya, Rector of the University of Santo Tomas, said among other things the following to the Philippine Commission on July 1, 1899:

> All secondary instruction in the Philippine Islands was under the University of Santo Tomas. Besides the private schools in Manila there were also some in the provinces, but all the colleges of secondary instruction were subject to Santo Tomas.

> There were primary schools in almost all the towns supported by the Government in which a very elementary instruction was given * * * reading, writing, catechism, and a little arithmetic.
>
> The Filipinos, as a general rule, have good memory but without great talent; they have no good talent.
>
> Almost all education in the Philippines was given by the religious orders, that is to say, the secondary and university instruction was maintained by the religious orders, and primary instruction by the curates of the towns.
>
> Among the Filipinos all is imitation. They lack originality. They were taught how to read and write Spanish but the majority of them learned it in a purely mechanical manner.
>
> The Indios were very averse to the Castilian language; those who knew how to speak it did not like to speak it. This was true in Manila as well as in its suburbs. Those who know Spanish prefer to speak their own language in their homes.

From Fray José M. Ruiz in his Memoria presented to the Philippine Exposition in Madrid in 1887, we take the following:

> The curate is a local inspector of public instruction, adviser of the gobernadorcillos, and president of the various local boards. The Indios see in them a father, a pastor, and a protector, and as such they have always been recognized by the Government of these Islands (p. 239).
>
> A great part of the Philippine inhabitants, that is to say, that which lives in the barrios and places more or less isolated and inaccessible, is about to be civilized (está casi por civilizar) (p. 247).

Referring to the mass of the people the same father says:

> The masters devoted as they are, save in a few honorable exceptions, to their proper interests, have *ignored* completely the instruction of these unhappy ones in their *religious* duties * * * and their children, given over to the pasture of work animals, are reared in the midst of the most stupid ignorance (p. 254).

Later the author adds:

> To give the Indio means of instruction and to place him in condition to benefit from it, and while this is not done, and *until now this has not been done* as we shall later show, is to concede rights to him who does not know how to appreciate what he deserves to the disgrace of the Spanish name and to the shame of the Spaniards in these Islands (p. 288).

Says the same Friar Ruiz:

> And altho they are inimical to going to schools (the Indios) and to sending their children, it is because it is *nothing but for wasting time* since they learn nothing * * *. Furthermore, the towns are so crowded with ignorant teachers that without consulting anybody they establish private schools paid for by the parents of the children. Thus they learn what little good and a great deal of bad which they possess, to whom they teach *Cartilla*, and something of reading and writing, utilizing as texts for both the books called *Corridos*, which are full of anachronisms, errors, and absurdities of all kinds * * *. They also learn something of the Catechism (p. 337).
>
> The places for the schools besides being bad are completely abandoned, and many are in ruins (p. 339).
>
> There is no order in the school, and each one goes in and out without permission whenever he pleases (p. 440).

Recognition of a Dominican

Fray José M. Ruiz very faithfully recognizes the lamentable state in which the so-called public instruction in the Philippines was found outside of Manila where things were not so bad. From his standpoint it was necessary to teach Spanish and at least to give to the Filipinos books in the dialects, from which they would learn the most elementary things of which they were ignorant, and Religion and Moral. The *Rueda*[5] translation would be better adding something about the Philippines and the grammar of his dialect in Spanish. Undoubtedly he wanted to say that the Spanish grammar should be translated into the dialects.

> If this is not done we believe that we would only lose time. With such measures in thirty years the Spanish language would be diffused among the children (pp. 440–441).
>
> For the same reason (distance and lack of roads) the boys and girls do not attend schools, and what little they know they learn from some ignorant teachers (maestrillos). People, ordinarily of bad life, escaped from other towns, some of whom are also quack doctors and bone-setters who at the same time that they are teaching the *Cartilla* and a little bit of the *Catechism* imbue the children with a thousand and one superstitions and all kinds of vices. The priest who at times goes, out of necessity, to attend to some one who is seriously ill, and very seldom visits them (the Indios) *ex-profeso*, the parochial districts being generally very large and their duties so numerous and urgent, can only in part remedy some of these evils.

---

[5] This book was printed in 1844. Today, in the year 1920, the seventh edition of the *Rueda* is sold in Manila and is used in some of the private schools. This edition is a reprint of the original edition without any correction so that in history Japan is not even mentioned, France is a kingdom, Prussian is separated from the rest of Germany; and in Spain, Isabela II is the one who still happily reigns. This is the famous book recommended by the priest who was interested in extending instruction in the Philippines.

The Filipino People

Now let us see what kind of people the Filipinos were. It is essential to know the psychology of the community. No opinion is so valuable for the present case than that of the missionary above cited, who says the following about the psychology of the Filipino.

> As a people who are ignorant and with but little culture, the Indios are bound to have considerable superstitious beliefs which they practice, unconsciously deceived by medicine men, who are the ones who keep alive these ridiculous traditions of their ancestors, without knowing the reasons for what they do (p. 261).
>
> They (the Indios) are deeply superstitious, a thing which is revealed in all their acts.

Citing the words of Dr. Lacalle, Father Ruiz says:

> To pretend that a people taking the first steps on the road of civilization, and that in their religious acts manifest themselves in their acts as religious, severe, cultured and real thinkers, is absurd in the extreme (p. 348).

And he adds what follows:

> We should not lose sight of the fact that the Indio is a child badly educated, but a big child completely developed in his passions. He acts not from conscience but from fear; he is moved not by reasons but by impressions; a friend of novelties and spectacles, he acts to the tune of the various impressions which he receives. Naturally he is inconstant and flighty, desiring one thing and another, now liking what he formerly disliked, without firmness nor stability in anything, without knowing many times what to like, nor what befits him. Such is the Indio briefly sketched.

The Filipino Spaniards

The Filipino Spaniards (españoles filipinos) are of two classes: some are immediate descendants of Spaniards, descendants of Filipino Spaniards, or also children of a Filipina mother and a peninsular father (p. 288).

Unfortunately, they have all the bad qualities of the Spaniard and the Indio, and lack that docility of character observed in the latter and the nobility and greatness characteristic of the former. They are of little heart, coward and mean besides being arrogant and choleric and are very rude with the Indios, whom they usually despise and maltreat in words and in deed, and frequently are stupid and troublesome.

From the Indios they learned all the superstitions, numerous, untrue, absurd fables which are traditional among them, and in a word, all their habits and customs. Thus they eat rice with their fingers and have marked fondness for the sweets and dirty foodstuffs of the Indios.

Since they are brought up with much petting and are not strictly punished, they make bad servants, disobedient, capricious, insolent, and foul-mouthed. The women are so lacking in modesty, and, since they have been reared in the atmosphere of abandon and laziness, they are useless for the management of the home and the family (pp. 289–290).

* * * Thus the men as well as the women, altho religious, are credulous and superstitious as the Indios themselves.

Such is the idea that can be given about the Filipinos (p. 290).

The Chinese half-breed is described in the same manner.

Literature for the Filipinos

The only literature accessible to the Filipinos of little culture and also to those of the better class consisted of *Corridos* which constitute the profane literature, and the *Pasión* and the *Novenas* which formed the religious reading. *Corridos*, *Pasiones*, and *Novenas* were printed in abundance, in cheap editions, in Spanish as well as in the dialects of the country.

The *Corridos* are stories in verse about historic events, falsified and fanciful, and love tragedies full of wonderful events mixed with divine prodigies and diabolical magics—all lengthy, exaggerated, puerile, and absurd in the extreme. None of the characters is native. All are Turks, Arabs, knights, errants, ambassadors, dukes, warriors in armor provided with magic arms and with balsams like the famous one of Fierabras, good Castilians and bad strangers. All the characters are antipodal to Philippine realities and with the semblance of the real and true being from unknown lands and prodigious races. The same is true with the scene of activities; wonderful lands, Palestine, the kingdom of Navarra, the Empire of Great Kahn, the Palace of Macedonia, and not only are they ignorant of, and do they falsify, the face of the earth, but the planetary system itself suffers a radical change. Palms and tamarind grow in the vicinities of Moscow; Palestine and Macedonia are covered with prairies like Norway and Switzerland, and whales appear in the Mediterranean. Events which begin in the morning in Macedonia and in the most natural manner in the afternoon of the same day in a palace of Babylonia, and a princess of Aragon captured early in the morning in Sicily discusses at midnight and without an interpreter with a Moro of Samarcanda.

The *Pasión*, a work in verse in the different Filipino dialects, is not only the passion of Christ, but it consists of a sort of abridged edition of sacred history.

The *Novenas* are religious booklets dedicated to a saint whose favor is invoked in order to obtain from God such and such favors. They consist of a system of prayers in relation to certain miracles with reflections about the saint, which are said every day for a period of nine consecutive days. To

Virgin Mary is attributed the origin of the *Novenas* because *she venerated the number 9* in memory of the fact that nine days it was when she was apprised of the incarnation of the divine Messiah, and also because of the nine months in which she carried Him in her virgin womb. (Novena to Jesús, María, and José, Manila, 1903, in the Exordium.)

The *Novenas* offer a very simple way of obtaining from heaven what is asked in them from a protector saint. If the sympathy and aid of a patron or a patroness whose mediation is implored is won, one can obtain everything, be it appertaining to earthly life or future life. It is a very easy means. It is like a magic ceremony with its ritual composed of praises and acts of humiliation, devotion, submission, admiration, and other propitiatory manifestations looking toward gaining the sympathy and the protection of the saint. This follows an enumeration of favors which may be requested and which are always attended to by God as demonstrated by the numerous examples which are mentioned with scrupulous care in the *Novena*. All the *Novenas* are published with ecclesiastical permit after the censorship of the prelate who examines scrupulously the writings to see if there is anything that is contrary to morals, good customs, and absolute orthodoxy. In a word, all are printed *with the necessary licenses*.

The prodigies mentioned in these *Novenas* compare very well with the enchantments, magics, and sorceries of the primitive Filipinos who invoked the propitiation of their divine spirits by means of ceremonies, sacrifices, charms, and incantations performed by their *mangkukulam* (witch), *babailanas*, and other prestidigitators, priests, medicine men, charmers, and fortune-tellers, which are referred to and are enumerated in the old chronicles written by the missionaries in the Philippines.

Substitution of "Unseen Powers"

All the fear of the mysterious as well as the belief of the Filipinos in unseen powers which took away life, attracted misfortunes, gave victory, or conduced to disaster was conserved, changing only the concepts that they had about the spirits that governed the affairs of life and the phenomena of nature. The patron saints recommended by the missionaries came to take the place of the ancient anitos representative of their past which they gave intervention in their idolatry in all the affairs of life.

When the missionaries preached their religion, they condemned the old Pagan superstitions but they taught new superstitions more powerful than the original, not only because of the prestige of the new patrons who are all members of a Celestial Court organized as an earthly aristocracy and headed by the same God, Creator of the Universe, but by communicating with God in the same tongue, which the ordinary man supposed was spoken by Him, which is the Latin tongue, in which the priests said their prayers and sang their hymns.

"Ensalmos"

The *Oremus*, the *Laus Deo*, *Agnus Dei*, *Deo Gracias*, *Nos cum prole pia*, *Benedicat Virgo Maria*, *Per omnia secula seculorum*, *Kyrie eleyson, Christe eleyson*, came under the category of enchantments (ensalmos) known by the terms *bolong* and *mantala* of the primitive *mangkukulam*, *mang̃hihikup*, *mananang̃isama*, etc. etc., of Philippine paganism. All of these Latin phrases acquired so great a prestige that they were looked upon as a form of irresistible invocation for conquering the divine will, and a certain ridiculous sect came to be known as the *Colorum*, which term originated from the wrong pronunciation of *secula seculorum* with which many Latin prayers ended, prayers which were incomprehensible but used due to the ignorance of many.

The phrase *agnus dei qui tolis pecata mundi* is used as an incantation in which every word more or less incomprehensible has a sacred character so that if one should say that he despises *qui tolis*, it would be considered a blasphemy because the *Qui Tolis* is something sacred or divine. A child after saying the *trisagio* said by way of protest: "I am tired of saying *kirileson* (Kyrie eleyson)." His mother then punished him for playing with the name of God. Another child who happened to name a dog Qui Tolis was corrected by his aunt, saying: "The name of God is never used for naming an animal."

Magic Invocations

All this constitutes a real array of magic invocation in the efficacy of which there is great confidence to avoid evil, ridding of danger, securing more good, and attaining some grace. As an example of the power of the invocations and what can be obtained by merely saying frequently "Jesús, María, y José" (Jesus, Mary, and Joseph), which constitutes the most "divine trinity on earth," the following cases are related: (*Novena a Jesús, María y José*, Manila, 1903).

A bad man walking in the middle of the night in front of the church of San Francisco in Cuzco, Peru, saw lights in the cemetery, and knowing it to be a funeral, went to the place to witness it. Presently he noted that there was a throne where Jesus Christ was found seated between Mary and Joseph. Then several demons appeared, each one with a book in his hand. One of them began accusing a bad woman from Buenos Aires. "Jesus," says the Novena, "pronounced a sentence against her of instant death and with it eternal perdition" (p. 7). The demon disappeared in order to execute the sentence. Another devil read from his book that in Chile there was another bad woman. "Jesus sentenced her to death and condemnation" (p. 8). The devil ran to carry out the sentence. Another one appeared accusing a bad man of Cuzco, and this man was precisely the same who tarried to witness the scene at the cemetery. "When the just *judge* was about to sentence him to death and condemnation, Blessed Mary and Joseph knelt before the divine Master, asking mercy on behalf of the accused, alleging that many times he invoked the holy names (Jesús, María y José). Jesus having denied pardon, his parents begged him anew, and seeing that they were not making headway toward securing pardon, the Blessed Virgin showed to her Blessed Son the breast from which He sucked, and the Patriarch Saint showed him the hands that maintained him thru his labors" (p. 8). Then Jesus conceded the pardon as a matter of grace which can only be characterized as material gratefulness (estómago agradecido).

Great Incentive to Crime

The invocation "Jesús, María y José" working as a magic formula saved that man who had no more merit than his ability to mention the names of the "trinity on earth." In the same *novena* there is a *consideration of this most marvelous favor*, and that is, that in order to obtain some reform in our lives in view of the favor conceded by Jesus, Mary, and Joseph to their devotee, *tho he be a confirmed sinner*, it was only necessary to imitate an invocation so frequently repeated in all his days of malice, the words "Jesús, María y José" (p. 10). The man in question had no other merit nor is he enjoined to have one. It is enough that he utters the magic invocation and that he does as he pleases in the belief of being free from punishment. What a great incentive this is to crime!

Another Notable Case

Another notable case of the effect of the same invocation is that of a Dominican friar called Fray Juan Masias, who for more than twelve years stayed in his dark cell in prayer. He was visited by many devils who pulled and pushed him, treating him very badly in words and in deed. But he was freed from them by saying "Jesus Savior, Mary, and Joseph, be with me." On other occasions the devils entered hurriedly and noisily catching him by the legs and dragged him from his room to the cloister. Some hit him and slapped him, others stepped on his stomach and on his head, still others scratched his face and sought to pluck his eyes, but invoking the names of Jesus, Mary, and Joseph, they (the devils) vanished and left him (p. 14). And the strangest part of it is that the friar made the invocation after suffering the consequences of the punishment above mentioned; so that, in other words, he condescended to allow the devils to have some fun for a while at his expense.

An Economical Diversion

The same friar "at other times while going to church in prayer, was caught by the devils and was taken; and they threw him up in the air so high that, passing above the roofs of the capitular hall which divides the first cloister from the next, he fell in the latter. There other devils were awaiting him and receiving him they threw him anew in the same manner so that he landed again in the principal cloister without hearing from him a word of protest or suffering until invoking the sacred names of Jesus, Mary, and Joseph, they left him (p. 15). Who on reading this would not envy a friar having a diversion so entertaining and so sane and economical? How can one help being grateful to the demons who received him in the other hall instead of letting him fall on the floor? With reference to these prodigies mentioned one reads in the same Novena the following considerations: "What trouble is there for us to habituate ourselves in repeating in our invocations the sweetest names of Jesus, Mary, and Joseph? (p. 27).

The Infernal Power

At every step this infernal power is amplified and magnified in these Novenas. Not only is the devil deemed among the enemies of the soul, together with our body and the entire humanity, but at every moment we tremble at his snares, we consider ourselves weak to resist him and even at times seemingly fearing that the self same God will not know how to defend Himself from the devil because at every step it is sought to awaken God and place him as a sort of guard against this infernal power. "Help us Lord from heaven, our strong liberator in this struggle with the powers of darkness; and as other times thou hast freed thy son, Jesus, from imminent peril of life, so now defend the Holy Church of God from the snares of their enemies and from all adversity, and keep each one of us under thy eternal protection." (Page 54, *Ofrecimiento al Santísimo Rosario*, Manila, 1905.)

Another Miracle

The following miracle shows clearly the work of the devil and shows at the same time that souls cannot be condemned so easily when a mortal beseeches the protection of a powerful patron. "A certain man," it is said in the Novena of San Vicente (p. 15), "gave his soul to the devil *with a certificate (cedula) signed by his own hand*, and hearing the Saint preach, implored him to ask that the demon return it. The Saint fell to praying, and made the devil come and ordered him to return the certificate to the man, having as witnesses of this miracle many thousands of persons."

Silliness of Some Saints

This foolish fear of the devil is a cause of many errors such as the one mentioned in the following miracle: "In Trayguerra, a simple lad hearing San Vicente preach on the ugliness of the demon, prayed God that a devil be shown him in order to fight. It happened that a poor, old woman was passing who was dumb from birth, was very ugly and poorly dressed, and had sickle in her hand. The lad, thinking that she was the devil, furiously assailed her, and taking away her sickle, cut off her hands, her ears, and her nose. The afflicted woman shouted but as she was dumb she could not make herself understood and only howled, and then the simpleton cut her up, saying: "Let them come and they will see what I do with the devils!" (p. 18, *Novena de San Vicente*). To believe that God permitted a similar infamy is a gross insult to God. True, the act is committed by a silly lad, but sillier still is the work of the saint in speaking of the physical ugliness of the demon, when according to the understanding of all, the demon is a spirit.

"In Taulada," says the *Novena* (p. 21), "two Moros passed in front of an image of San Vicente, one of whom took off his hat and the other did not. The latter paid dearly for it for in that instant, without knowing from whom, he was slapped, fell to the ground, and had fever from which he died." It was wonderful how it was known that it was a slap, and the miracle could not have been more cruel, not especially because of the insignificance of the *fault* committed, inasmuch as it dealt with a Moro who did not believe nor did he understand this Christian superstition.

A devout one who was wont to go to Saint Filomena asks protection against the devil (*Novena*, p. 22) and says: "Satan like a hungry lion makes a round about turn; his ministers vie with one another to put me down. I with my frailty am also the enemy of my own soul * * *."

As I said the *Novenas* are used to implore a divine mercy, utilizing the intervention of a saint or a virgin to secure some necessity or a simple affair in life.

There is nothing more inspiring than to know the news about the origin of the *Novena de San Antonio de Padua* which "is said to be revealed by the same saint * * * and the devout ones can follow it confident of obtaining thru his intermediation whatever they desire" (*Novena de San Antonio*, p. 5). "The same San Antonio revealed to a devout woman the way of doing it" (p. 6).

He Who Asks Shall Receive

The *Novena of María de los Dolores*, Manila, 1905, is "for obtaining what is desired in any affair of the soul or for the good of the body."

The *Novena of San Vicente de Ferrer* "altho it can be made in the home, it is much better to do it in the church *because there he who asks shall receive and he who looks shall find*, as *the Lord himself said*" (p. 5 of the *Novena*, Manila, 1917).

San Ramon Nonato is: "Patron of the work of the laborers and their *livestock*; wonderful antidote against pestilence; universal refuge for the cure of all diseases and pains; singular protector of the women who invoke him in their dangerous hours of giving birth, and of the sterile ones who seek the comfort of his protection." This is what is said in the frontispiece of his *novena*, Manila 1918. "By merely invoking his name or by adoring his saintly relic, and by drinking the water where it is passed, the saint can accomplish thousands of wonders" (p. 6).

"I," says one devout woman, "have such faith in and experience with, San Ramon that whatsoever I ask God thru him was always secured or obtained, and for the sake of truth, I swear and confirm the same" (*Novena*, p. 15).

A form of great persuasive virtue to obtain the divine will and to win from it what is desired is to pray the Trisagio. It seems that during a period of great geologic and meteorologic commotions experienced in Constantinople in the year 447 (*Trisagio Seráfico*, Manila, 1889, p. 7), it happened that "a child of tender age was carried to the winds, all those encamped being eye witnesses, until he could be seen no more. After a long time he returned to earth in the same manner that he went up and stated in the presence of the Patriarch, of the Emperor, and of the wondering multitude, that he heard the angels sing this concert: 'Holy God, Holy Strong, Holy Immortal, have mercy upon us.' (Santo Dios, santo fuerte, santo inmortal, tened misericordia de nosotros.)" The child immediately thereafter died. The Emperor ordered that all should repeat this sacred canticle and that moment the earthquakes ceased and the meteorological disturbances stopped. Hence, "the use of the Trisagio as a form for invoking the Holy Trinity in dangerous fatal times" (p. 78). Among other things the following is tacitly asked in the Trisagio: "Of thy ire and anger, Lord and triune free us. Of the snares, nearness of the demon; of all ire, hate and bad will; of all plagues or epidemics, hunger, storms; of our enemies and their machinations free us" (pp. 20–21).

Reminders of Cannibalism

Altho the Trinity is composed, as everybody knows, of the Father, Son, and Holy Ghost, and in the Trisagio the three persons are invoked and asked at the same time, nevertheless there are other forms of securing the divine favor, invoking separately only one of the persons of the Trinity. Thus in the *Novena of Jesus Sacramentado*, the *Father* is asked by means of the intercession of the Son, or in other words, by only a viscera of the Son or an organ of his body, the heart, or more properly the Sacred Heart of Jesus. "The eternal Father has complacency," says the *Novena* (p. 6), "in that it is asked in the name of the Heart of his beloved Son * * *." "The Father Eternal said so directly to the venerable Mary of the incarnation" (pp. 6–7). "Ask me thru the heart of my only begotten Son, and thru it I shall hear thee and thou shalt obtain all that thou wouldst ask * * *." Jesus said to his wife Margaret (esposa Margarita): "I ask you that on Friday immediately before the Corpus festivity, you particularly devote yourself to the *worship of my heart*" (p. 7).

The adoration of the heart is not symbolic; it is the real heart that is adored: "they shall adore with greater frequency, to Jesus transsubtantiated, and in him, to his Divine Heart" (p. 7). "His Novena will be made before an image of Jesus or to His Sacred Heart" (p. 10). The devout one, carrying his adoration almost to a point of the revival of atavic cannibalism, says to Jesus: "O, thou owner of mine! Give me thine body and with it thine heart *that I may eat it*!" (para que le coma) (p. 12).

There is a *Novena* dedicated to Saint Angel Custodio (Manila, 1897), who is the "Angel delegated by God to be at our side, and exercise with us the loving offices of a careful tutor, a loving governor, a loving preceptor, a faithful conductor, and an intimate and true friend * * *" (p. 6). "No saint in heaven interests himself more in our soul and in our business than the holy Guardian Angel" (p. 6). His intervention is so useful and "he not only transmits what is asked but modifies our petitions when he knows that some of our petitions might bring us some spiritual or corporal evil" (p. 7). "It is therefore the best guarantee against any error of ours, and naturally it makes a sense of responsibility absolutely useless."

Second Christ

Saint Domingo de Guzman is one of the most powerful lawyers in heaven. In his *Novena* (Manila, 1913), he is called the *precursor of Christ*, altho in reality he came to the world twelve centuries after Christ (p. 5). "In the chastity, color, and figure of his body, and in the eloquence of his spirit, he was the one *most like Christ*" (p. 7). He was very celebrated in all manners of prodigies and miracles, both on earth and in heaven, among men as well as among beasts, among the living as well as the dead" (p. 9). One day Virgin Mary appeared to him and "holding him by the hand said to him that she loved him so tenderly, that *if the Divine Lady were a mortal*, she would not be able to live except in his presence, and would have died by the violence of the great love that she had for him * * *" (p. 10). Later Virgin Mary, not satisfied with such erotic manifestations, married him (le desposó consigo) in the presence of her husband Christ (esposo de Cristo), and of many blessed ones in heaven" (pp. 11–12), resulting that Jesus, besides being the son of Mary, is also her husband, so that with Saint Joseph, Saint Domingo was the third husband of Mary. The Eternal Father communicated to Saint Catalina de Sena that Christ and Domingo were his two special sons * * *." Christ proceeded from the mouth of the Eternal Father, staying at his right, and Saint Domingo proceeded from the breast of the same Eternal Father, at his right on his feet in glory" (p. 15). With such antecedents one can readily understand how "Christ promised to concede to him all that he would ask on behalf of his devotees" (p. 15), so that the power of the Saints is unlimited. In verse it is said of him:—

> You can do everything in heaven
> being husband of Mary;
> Who so confides in thee (Domingo)
> give him health and comfort.
> You have faithfully and unceasingly
> defended the church (p. 35).

> Pues podeis tanto en el Cielo,
> Siendo esposo de María;
> Domingo, al que en vos confía,
> Dadle salud y consuelo" (p. 35).
> Fuesteis can que con desvelo
> a la Iglesia defendida * * *" (p. 35).

The *can* is referred to here because while the mother was pregnant it (the foetus, el feto) was manifested to her in the form of a dream and in the figure of a dog with a lighted ax in his mouth (p. 6).

Promises of the Virgin

The *Novena* to the Virgin of the Rosary begins with an enumeration of the FIFTEEN PROMISES of the Virgin to the devotees of the Rosary. In the first she promises to grant whatever special grace is asked of her. He who prays the rosary will be converted if he is a sinner, and in *any event* will be admitted to life eternal. "All that is asked of her will be secured quickly" (p. 4).

The list of miracles performed by the image of the Virgin of the Rosary is endless and occupies all the pages from 37 to 90 of the *Novena*. Not only does the image perform miracles but her skirt as well as the oil that burns in her lamp, and the water where her hands are washed, or any rosary or object touched by her skirt or her image also accomplish miracles (p. 9).

In the *Novena* of Saint Joseph (Manila, 1910), after reminding him of his relation with God, it is affirmed that "there is no protection more efficacious for securing all that is asked than his" (p. 7). "Necessitating everything from the divine favor it is sure that none shall fail who confident will seek the protection of Saint Joseph" (p. 29). "Saint Joseph assists the needy, gives health to the sick, consoles the afflicted, sends rains, freezes ice, multiplies fruits, favors in storms, on the roads, and among the drowning * * *. Finally there shall be none who trusting in the same will not receive that which is asked."

To the Holy Child of Cebu, an image which was left in that city by the companions of Magellan, went the Cebuanos before their conversion to Catholicism to ask rain "carrying him in a procession to the seashore and submerging it in the water and thus secure the rain that they needed so much." (*Novena al Santísimo Nombre*, Malabón, 1895, p. 5). Nevertheless, the immersion in the sea water is a recourse which may be said to be resorted to only in extreme cases because a verse in that novena says:

> Si acaso no conseguían
> las aguas porque os rogaban,
> al mar, Oh Niño, os llevaban,
> y en las aguas os metían;
> y así el agua que pedían,
> otorgaba vuestro amor" (p. 29).

> If they failed to get the waters they prayed for, to the sea, Oh Child, they carried thee and put thee in the water, so that thy love conceded the water they asked.

The better known miracles by the Holy Child took place from 1618 to 1675. Since then nothing in the *Novena* that is memorable is registered. Nevertheless, the novena confirms that "the Holy Child performs continually" miracles (p. 15), and to "him go all the citizens of Cebu, Bohol, Leyte, Samar, and Mindanao to kiss his sacred feet and venerate him and commend to him their necessities and misfortunes, asking relief in their sickness, assistance in their voyages, and protections in all the events of life" (pp. 15–16).

The certainty of finding what is sought in the *novenas* is assured in reference to Saint Roque. "The exercise of this *novena*," it is said (p. 3, *Novena*, Manila, 1910), "offers us a means of *compelling* (obligar) this glorious saint to secure of God what we ask." To be rid of epidemics—which has its origin in the corruption of the air—we must have recourse to San Roque with fervent prayers" (p. 3). By the side of the corpse of the saint a letter was found which was supposed to have been written by God, which reads: "Those afflicted with plague who implore the favor of Roque will find health" (p. 5). The intervention of Saint Roque is exclusively in favor of the Catholics. Who so makes his *novena* says the following:

"I implore thee that by the merits of this glorious Saint, thou freest us all who assist to this cult and *to all the Catholics* of the Kingdom of Spain and of these Islands of all pestilential diseases which might take away our lives"

(p. 13). Since the Catholics of the United States are not included here, the Bureau of Health ought to remember that such citizens together with those who are not Catholics who inhabit the Philippines do not enjoy the anti-pestilential protection of Saint Roque.

Superstition and Crime

In his notable study on Criminal Anthropology of the Philippines, Dr. Sixto de los Angeles (p. 119) says:

> The easy credulity fomented by the over-development of religious fanaticism, has constituted from the beginning to this day one of the defects unfortunately so widespread still among the native inhabitants of the country * * *. Devoted to their inherited traditions and customs and lacking in adequate opportunities to acquire proper knowledge, the mass of the people have to adhere as it is logical and natural, to their beliefs, which by their not requiring any effort to understand are imbedded and deeply rooted in a spontaneous manner in their minds. *As it is shown in our annals of the judiciary, superstition occupies a notable place among the factors of criminality in this country.*

The superstitions to which Doctor de los Angeles alludes are not only those of the old paganism of the Filipinos which the missionaries after more than three centuries have not succeeded in completely eradicating. The superstitions referred to in this work are those brought here by the same missionaries, and which they have easily succeeded in implanting in the conscience of the Filipinos naturally disposed to credulity by means of the efficient and generous distribution of the *novenas* and other booklets of devotion.

Since until the coming of the Americans the instruction in the Philippines was always and exclusively religious, and was directed by the Roman priests, the persistence of these old superstitions are evident proofs of the failure of religious education. As an excuse missionaries will perhaps attribute this to the invincible rudeness of the Filipinos, which we shall admit for courtesy's sake and to avoid discussions. But what is all-important is not that they were unable to take out something (of the superstitions), out of the supposed hardheadedness of the Indio, but the tremendous wealth of superstition which for more than three centuries these missionaries inculcated (han hecho penetrar) in that same head to the detriment of his mentality and his morality.

Lack of Will

The sinner lacking in will to control his evil deeds says to Jesus, washing his hands in the divine intervention and giving proof of his lack of due sense of responsibility: "Is it possible, sweet Saviour of souls, that, converting so many every day, *alone in my perdition*, thou mayest show thyself indifferent?" (p. 13). This is a part of a prayer made by no less a person than His Holiness, Pope Gregory VII, in his *Devout Exercise of the Passion of Christ*, Manila, 1905.

It is said also to the Virgin: "Cleanse, thou Immaculate Virgin, my heart of all sin and take away from me all that may be unpleasant in thy purest eyes! Purge my soul of all earthly love and affections" (pp. 10–11, *Corona Franciscana de la Virgen María*, Manila, 1902).

By the intercession of Saint Francis, the devout one asks of God that "I completely subdue my disorderly passions, powers, and senses," so "that I may subject my thoughts, measure my words, and direct my work to the greatest perfection," and "that thou mayest soften the hardness of my heart" (pp. 18, 20, and 21 of the *Novena of Saint Francis de Asis*, Manila, 1905).

Frightened by the machinations of Satan the devout one to Saint Filomena asks (p. 23, *Novena*): "She obtains from the Lord that which destroys more and more the powers of my enemies, the devils, and that *I be saved in spite of myself.*"

The guidance of Saint Filomena is invoked by saying (p. 25, *Novena*): "See to it that I also be chaste according to my station, and that my mouth will not utter those words which according to St. Paul, should not be said among the faithful."

To Saint Anna, mother of Mary, the devout one says: "Interest thyself therefore, my Saint, that I may be granted patience in my adversities, tolerance of wrongs, and, in everything, a tranquil mind" (*Novena*, Manila, 1893, p. 10). Also the following prayer is directed: "Put forth therefore your effort, my Saint, with thy sacred grandson, Jesus, that every imperfection and bad desire may be taken from our hearts, that we may pardon for love of God all wrongs."

It is not possible to cultivate a sense of dignity or self-respect itself when doctrines are disseminated such as these, which result from the following examples in the Novena of Santa Rosa de Lima.

Carried by her humility, she made a mere servant step on her lips (p. 10). "She loved ridicules more than worldly honors" (p. 102). * * * and she desired so much that all others considered her the worst in the world, that she merited being in hell, and that it was her proper place because of her sins. If any body happened not to know her and that she was considered innocent, she would say "nobody knows me, I alone know what I am" (p. 11). "Hearing once that they praised her as being virtuous she felt so bad that she fainted" (p. 11).

In a prayer to Saint Filomena (*Novena*, p. 16), it is said to the saint asking her protection: "My sins made me less than angels, very inferior to the beasts, since these do not forget the manger of their master, and in their own way they are grateful for their food, and I have forgotten the house of God * * *." Not only self ridicule comes out of these things, but lack of logic in attributing to the gratitude of the beasts their return to their manger, when it is clear that the motive that prompts them is simply hunger.

The Ire of God

The natural phenomena are looked upon thru ignorance as manifestations of the divine wrath which would not have taken place if no one among humanity had not provoked them by their conduct. Saint Thomas Aquinas, who with reason is considered as the most scientific man of his period, believed firmly that the thunder, lightning, and the storms were punitive manifestations of God enraged against men. "From his fear of God, the saintly doctor had an unearthly fear of thunder and tempests, who as a reverent child feared to see wrath in the face of the Father, hoping only that those tempests were not provoked by his sins" (*Milicia Angélica*, Manila, 1907, p. 21).

The blind fear of Saint Thomas led him to conceive a blind justice of the divinity, because of his sins God released the tempests and gave lightning which naturally hurt and molested a great number of persons who suffered by reason of the sins of the saint. To the simple believer, when the wise saint thought and believed in that manner, there was no reason for rejecting the explanation, much less to suspect that to punish justly the sinners was not an act of justice nor of common sense.

Lack of Logic

Logical mentality cannot be developed when the absurd is fomented and cultivated, especially when it is presented under the false veneer of religion, when it is founded on a purely puerile and simple superstition.

In the life of Saint Vicente Ferrer, according to his novenas, the following miracles are referred to, and there is no doubt that he who believes in them cannot really cultivate the faculties of his intelligence.

> In Valencia a servant of Count de Faura, who was born deaf and without tongue, was that way for many years, and adoring one day the miracle of Saint Vicente, was cured of

> his deafness, his tongue *grew*, and thenceforward spoke (p. 17).
>
> A woman gave birth to a piece of meat (pedazo de carne) without a human aspect. It was offered to Saint Vicente giving a mass, and at the Epistle, it already had head; at the Gospel, it had arms; and at the Consecration, it had legs, and finally a beautiful child was evolved. The same happened with another woman of Toledo (p. 34).
>
> In Lisbon there lived a woman well-known for being quite ugly and was the object of ridicule on the part of all who saw her. She went to San Vicente and one morning she became very fortunate and beautiful, from which the women of Lisbon became so devout to San Vicente that those in Valencia did not excel them (p. 27).
>
> A merchant left once for a fair and meanwhile the wife committed an indiscretion (una fragilidad) for which she remained * * *. She came and appeared repentant to San Vicente and the same went to the road whereon the husband returned with some horses, and startled them by means of a cloak and thus dispersed them. Then the husband lost time to gather his horses so that when he returned to his house his wife had time to flee from him, thus saving herself from the consequences of her fault.

Thus with the greatest freedom an immoral and grotesque act is related in which the innocent husband is left out and takes no step to have just punishment meted, and the saint with his cloak commits a deviltry only fit for urchins of the brook.

It is said that San Ramon takes such a deep interest in the misfortunes and pains of his devotees, and is so extremely compassionate "that his images perspire thru the affliction of his devotees" (p. 12). "An image of the Saint perspired so copiously at one time that a devout woman suffered and the veil with which she covered herself was stained; and some handkerchiefs wet in his perspiration relieved headaches marvelously" (p. 21).

Saint Roque has the power of stopping the spread of epidemics. "His protection is what preserves us from plague and other sufferings or diseases, which, having their origin in the corruptions of the air, which should conserve our life, causes death" (p. 3).

The Height of Absurdity

Is it possible to invent or suppose greater absurdities than those here mentioned? Nevertheless, in order not to prolong this address, I shall only present a few of the cases which are cited in abundance in these little booklets (opusculos), distributed in great profusion among our people. What logic, what reasoning can we expect of minds nurtured with such absurdities, fed up with fakes of such puerile nature that one can hardly believe them to have been narrated by men of simple common sense?

> The mattress where San Vicente died has become possessed of the virtue of making miracles; by merely lying on it on different occasions over 400 sick persons afflicted with various diseases became well (p. 32).

One time when San Antonio de Padua preached on the seashore it happened "that the fishes to whom he preached came out of the water and heard him with all attention." No devotee ever doubts the coming out of fishes, nor does he interests himself in the solution of the physical, physiological, linguistic, and especially logical aspects of such an event, but the Novena to the Saint confirms it so (p. 20).

This lecture would be unduly prolonged if I were to mention all the absurdities that appear in the *Novenas* of which I have quite a collection, which constitute a real array of documents of positive usefulness for the history of the superstition which I have scarcely touched upon here. With what has been said there is enough to explain the origin of the immorality, the real cause of the predisposition to vice, the absence of a sense of responsibility, the natural explanation of what incomprehensible character formed of a mixture of sentiments which the missionaries have contributed to the Filipino, Indio, Spaniard, and Chinese, all influenced by the injurious spirit which pervades all that literature which is completely antagonical to reason. Such, and not the lay education, is responsible for this evil.

I am not here to formulate theories or to speak of a capricious hypothesis. Before an audience such as this which I have the honor to address, I need to weigh the value of my words and of my judgment. For this reason I have cited facts, repeating the exact words, not of the profane literature composed of the anonymous *Corridos* whose detrimental influence is well known, but the authentic texts of *Novenas authorized by the ecclesiastical censorship for not containing anything contrary to sane morals*, as it is said in the permits granted for their printing.

Nor have I thought for a moment of mixing religion in my criticism; nor is it in my power to vary the results or consequences that may result from the facts mentioned in the *Novenas*, which are the literature responsible for this state of puerile mentality, absolutely inadequate for an understanding of morals, composed of matter that paralyzes, rather than bring out, progress.

Morals is nothing but the triumph over one's self, thru which man does what he should and not what he wishes. In the immoral man there is no struggle between two tendencies, one against evil and the other against good. There is only the instinctive tendency; there is no rational control in opposition. What mastery over self does a man have who for the purpose of controlling his habit of dirty and obscene speech seeks the intervention of a saint? Lacking in will, dispossessed of any idea of struggle with himself, how can he triumph over himself? Slave to his own passions it might have seemed that the only thing that might control him was the punishment in store in future life; but this fear does not preoccupy him in the least since at the same time that he is threatened with eternal fire he is told the manner of evading it without ceasing to do evil.

Immorality of the Novenas

These *Novenas* contain pernicious teachings for society whose moral foundation consists in the development of the individual qualities such as industry, fulfillment of duty, respect of law, struggle with one's own instincts and passions which require above all else the mastery over one's self. Not only are these social obligations not taught nor mentioned but there is a real stimulus toward all that is bad, assuring to the criminal, to the sinner, that he will be pardoned, that he will be free from punishment, that however badly he may act and however sinful he may be, without the least effort, with the greatest ease and naturalness, he will obtain what he wishes and will triumph on earth as well as in the other life.

On the other hand, the individual is terrorized by the influence of evil, always tending to push him on to the road of vice and ignominy; he is inspired with blind confidence by placing on his side a Guardian Angel who never leaves night and day, who supports him, who guides him "his (the Guardian Angel's) intervention being so useful that he modifies that which we asked of God when he knows that our petitions might bring us some spiritual or bodily ill."

What idea of justice can one conceive when he remembers the spectacle that was witnessed by that gentleman in the cemetery of Cuzco? Not only are Mary and Joseph presented as interceding with all energy for the salvation of the criminal for the mere reason that he invoked their names, but they remain unmoved and do nothing to soften the cruelty of Jesus Christ when He condemns to sudden death and eternal condemnation the two unfortunate sinful women. They did not invoke the name of Mary and Joseph who only seem to have pity on their clients and work with the same partiality of a Nacionalista or Democrata demagogue.

And what significance does a law have which does not admit nor prosecute polygamy when so many virgins are wives of Jesus who expect the other life in order that they may deliver themselves to Him as their husband? What about Mary, wife of the Father, of her own son, of Joseph, and Saint Domingo?

Mr. Ignacio Villamor in his report to the Committee on Infant mortality, written when he was Attorney-General, refers to various cases of murder of persons considered as bewitched and as such were sacrificed for being fanatics.

The lad of Trayguerra who assailed the ugly woman for mistaking her for the devil himself after hearing a sermon of San Vicente, is absolutely of the same nature as those possessed of the *asuang* referred to by Mr. Villamor.

And what shall be said of the protection of San Isidro invoked by the agriculturists? He gave an example of neglect of his duties as a farmer, because instead of plowing the land, doing the work for which he was paid by his master, he spent the day praying. Thru a miracle, an angel took hold of the plow, guided the bulls while the saint prayed and did not work. And right here in our midst, confident in San Isidro, the people of the field sleep, hoping that the angels shall do the work for them! How can you condemn laziness when the angels protect it? And how can you preach the doctrine of "earning bread by the sweat of your brow" when the labor that sweat presupposes is unnecessary?

Without connection whatsoever with the Bureau of Education of the Government of the Philippine Islands, I have spoken in the manner that I have just done, not to defend the lay schools of an unjust and unjustifiable accusation; not to attack any persons or any religious or political ideals, but to contribute to the eradication of one of the bases, one of the strongest causes of criminality, of corruption, of formation of individuals who are useless and detrimental to society: *superstition*. And, gentlemen, it is not a superstition that is only to be laughed at. Not by any means. It is a ridiculous and even absurd superstition, it is true, but it is a tragic and dangerous because it offers to the wicked, the criminal, the imbecile, the means of triumphing in life, of obtaining what they want, giving them the means of avoiding punishment, making fun here on earth of the justice of men, and securing from God the pardon from eternal condemnation thru the simple means of invoking the name of a saint, or thru the medium of a Latin word which, acting as a sort of open sesame opens wide to the devotee the gates of heaven.

The Lamentable Error of the Bishop of Cebu

The prelate who accused the public schools in the form above mentioned has committed a lamentable error. For my part, I can say that the accusations awakened in me a desire to investigate the causes of immorality and of the perversion of customs which the said prelate, and we with him, all regret. According to those who have studied the mentality of the majority of our people, it is evident that superstition is the enemy which we all have to combat and that is the cause of many of the moral errors which we observe. The regular friars as well as the secular clergy confess that the mass of the people still finds itself subject to the superstition inherited from our predecessors—the superstition which could be called genuinely Philippine, that which comes from the old belief in the *nunu*, in the *asuang*, the anito and all the spirits of the old idolatry preached before the implantation of Catholicism by the Spanish missionaries.

Failure of the Missionaries

According to their own confessions, these missionaries, after three centuries of preaching, have failed to eradicate those superstitions incrustated in the conscience of the people. We must accept their declaration as a faithful recognition of the failure of their religious mission. I am not interested in, nor do I discuss, the religious point of view, but the importance of superstition in social life, its pernicious influence upon the evolution of morality. What undoubtedly results from the narratives contained in that literature which constituted the only reading of the people is the promotion of ignorance spreading in a very effective manner all the superstitions aforementioned and *adding to them a wealth of errors which unfortunately governs the mentality of the mass of the people.*

Not only the so-called Indios the ones concerned; the sons of the Spaniards of pure blood or those mixed with *Indios* as well as the Chinese mestizos are also accused of these superstitions. All these, all of us Filipinos, are included among the individuals infected with the leprosy of superstition fomented by the absurd miracles of the *Novenas* and it cannot be said that it is an evil particularly of the Filipino race but also the inhabitants of the Philippines in general.

In order that education be useful it has to form in the individual the *sense of responsibility* thru the free exercise of reason. The fulfillment of duty shall be its objective and in order to obtain this goal, it is highly necessary to develop the *will* in man with which he shall fight the animal instincts, the sentimental impulses, all that is contrary to the dictates of reason.

Logical mentality (mentalidad lógica), to know what we should do and to enable us to plan out a just route that we should follow; *will* (voluntad) to enable us to exalt the dictates of reason above the impulses of our own desires: such is the object of lay education, the education in the so-called godless schools, here in the schools of the Government as in the college of Beata Imelda directed by the Dominican fathers under the norm of Japanese ideas translated in imperative laws, situated in Taihoku, capital of Formosa.

The reading of the so-called miracles of the type that I have before cited makes the impossible appear possible, thanks to mysterious influences which are easy to secure, not thru industry, but simply thru unworthy and low means and reproved by good morals such as humiliation, adulation, and propitiation. A benefit is not asked or expected thru some positive good that we do, thru fulfillment of duty out of which results a positive good which is a right; resort is had by means of favor, by gaining the benevolence of a saint, making him believe that he is liked, adored, and admired, seeking to exalt his vanity and, thru his mediation, gain the good will of God, not as a benefit conferred directly to him who asks, but in consideration of the merits of the mediator. Nothing can be imagined that is more immoral, more primitive, more contemptible. The celestial court turns out to be a court more corrupt than those of the autocrats condemned by history: the court of the Khans, the Sultans, the Bysantine Emperors, Mungols, Persians, Tartars, all the barbarians who have abused humanity and who have personified injustice and justified revolution and massacres.

A society whose members expect everything thru favoritism does not know what emulation is; when an individual finds a means as simple as that offered in the *Novenas* to secure what he desires following the line of least resistance, does not resort to the exercise of any noble activity, and, consequently, cannot perfect his faculties nor use them; an individual who expects to attain the absurd and improbable cannot know the existence of immutable laws which rule the universe; the individual who expects to secure *what he wants* thru the medium of a celestial patron cannot conceive the God of Justice nor can he really be a useful member of society.

Favor, propitiation, exception, protection, grace, preference, predilection, are incompatible with what a God should be, with the Ideal of civilization, with the supreme aspiration of humanity which is *Justice*.

Disastrous Results

Those who believe in the absurd miracle (milagrería absurda), protector of the fools, accomplice of the lazy, of the gamblers, of thieves, of all who, thru its means, seek to secure what they desire—those are the criminals that fill our jails and who die in the gallows; those are the ones, who, armed with their *anting-anting*, *talisman*, rosary, scapulary, bones of saints, or shark's teeth, fight with the police, commit outrages, upset order, confident in their triumph because of the protection of their celestial *pintakasi*. Such is the product not of the schools without god but of god without schools, impossible and paradoxical, whose power manifests itself in capricious methods and in the exercise of prestidigitation. Those individuals are in truth the natural products of that superstition preached, diffused, and presented to the ignorance of people who have come to the point of fearing neither God nor devil and who know that the infernal punishment only is meted to him who does not wear a rosary around his neck or does not confide in a *pintakasi*, who guarantees eternal salvation because *God does not permit that the worshiper of one of His devotees be condemned.*

What kind of citizen can an individual be in society who laughs at punishment using the easy means of a celestial lawyer. How can terrors of hell infuse fear in him when he knows that thru the medium of a powerful lawyer, God finds himself *obliged* (forzado) to pardon him. And when a man knows the way of evading divine justice, it is clear that, in order for him to escape human justice, he will resort to appealing to the mercy of the judge, to evade compliance with the law, to the non-fulfillment of any duty, and to live only to enjoy his rights; he will resort, in dealing with human authorities, to the use of the same methods of propitiation, adulation, prevarication, humiliation, and deception which dominated the same God and triumphed over the power of the devil!

Never will it be possible for a superstitious man, especially if he is of the type that we have just analyzed, become a useful citizen. Such is the type which unfortunately is the product of an education of three centuries...!

The parochial schools (escuelas religiosas) have given their fruit; the lay schools (laicas) have also borne fruitage. The youths who graduate from the latter are undoubtedly not without defects; but they are not poisoned or forever led astray by that brutalizing superstition sown by native and foreign impostors. None of those youths will assail ruthlessly an ugly old woman mistaking her for a devil; he will not dream of flying in the air launched like a balloon by an army of devils. None shall believe that a piece of meat shall be transformed into arms, legs, and heads as a mass offered to a *pintakasi* progresses; much less can such youth conceive a Jesus Christ that would weaken at the sight of a chest that his mother Virgin Mary would show to remind him of his weak memory of God would forget; nor will he excuse himself of a wrong committed against a companion of the other sex on the pretext that he does not have with him the girdle of the Angelic Militia; much less will he believe that, in spite of a criminal life, he will be able to secure eternal salvation provided only he has taken the precaution of repeating at every turn the invocation of the so-called Trinity on Earth.

That lay education will not produce individuals who trust in protection or recommendation to progress and triumph on earth. The lay education is wholly democratic and will not be capable of committing the same faults of those who, by not following their education, seek to employ in the affairs of life those means recommended in the *Novenas* in order to obtain what is desired by means of the help of the powerful, secured by means of requests, protestations of love, and promise of eternal devotion.

That mental conformation created by the diffusion of this superstitious spirit is an obstacle, an insuperable barrier set up against the development of the moral sense. We shall sow principles of morality as the farmer who sows in the fields the seeds properly selected which will not grow unless the soil is adequate. Sane morals is founded upon the basis of reason; when this foundation is lacking, the moral taught will be like a trec that is rootless and lifeless. It is not possible that a school without god (escuela sin Dios) or the one with god can make the seed of morals grow upon a soil prepared by the school of superstition, of magic, and of sorcery. We have to prepare the soil cultivating reason and creating the logical sense.

I will only insist on things which only need to be presented before our common sense to be judged as they merit.

The Public School

Permit me now to express first of all my gratitude to the Assistant Director, Mr. Osias, who had the kindness to honor me with an invitation to speak at this conference. Now, I wish to express to you my thanks for your kind attention. Lastly, I desire to make one declaration: Every time I referred to the new generation, I did not want to mention only the youth educated in the lay schools of the Government, but all the youth educated in modern ideas, all the men and women of whatever age who, throwing aside the weighty burden of the Legacy of Ignorantism (Le gado del Ignorantismo), have accepted modern ideas, have modified their mentality, have been modernized, thanks to the example of, and the contact with, the representatives of American democracy. All the change, all the economic, moral, social, and political transformation effected in the Filipino people, and which none denies nor anyone can deny, reveals progress, and that progress is not the result of the *Legacy of Ignorantism* but the natural consequence of the régime of liberty, industry, work and logical mentality which governs our public schools and orients our social life.

To the Department of Education, to all the teachers of both sexes—Americans and Filipinos—I express my profound gratitude for the splendid manner in which they are complying with the duty entrusted to them by America and by the Philippines.

9 789361 384745

Printed by Libri Plureos GmbH in Hamburg,
Germany